MIRACLE NUTRIENT

Hundreds of scientific studies and thousands of clinical applications have documented that Coenzyme Q10, synthesized in every living cell of the human body, may be one of the greatest 20th century medicinal advances for the treatment of heart disease. Within these pages, one of the nation's most innovative cardiologists documents the proven benefits of this simple nutrient in a wide variety of clinical cardiac conditions from congestive heart failure and high blood pressure, angina and arrhythmia, to its role in successful cardiac surgery.

ABOUT THE AUTHOR

Stephen T. Sinatra, M.D., F.A.C.C. is a board-certified cardiologist, a certified bioenergetic psychotherapist, a fellow of the American College of Cardiology, Director of Medical Education at the Manchester Memorial Hospital and Assistant Clinical Professor of Medicine at the University of Connecticut School of Medicine. For over two decades, Dr. Sinatra has helped patients prevent and reverse heart disease utilizing conventional medical treatments as well as complementary nutritional and psychological therapies at his New England Heart Center in Manchester, Connecticut.

The author of *Heartbreak and Heart Disease* and other bestselling books, Dr. Sinatra serves as editor for *HeartSense*, a monthly newsletter devoted to healing the heart. He is at work on a larger, more comprehensive book on the many health benefits of Coenzyme Q10.

Coenzyme Q10 and the Heart

A miracle nutrient for the prevention and successful treatment of heart disease

Stephen T. Sinatra, M.D., F.A.C.C.
author of *Heartbreak and Heart Disease*

KEATS PUBLISHING

LOS ANGELES

NTC/Contemporary Publishing Group

For the late cardiologist, Dr. Per Lansjoen,
a brilliant and courageous physician who continued to research and
report on the clinical benefits of CoQ10 despite the tremendous
disapproval of his colleagues.

Coenzyme Q10 and the Heart is intended solely for informational and educational purposes and not as medical advice. Please consult a medical or health professional if you have questions about your health.

COENZYME Q10 AND THE HEART

Published by Keats
A division of NTC/Contemporary Publishing Group, Inc.
4255 West Touhy Avenue, Lincolnwood (Chicago), Illinois 60646-1975, U.S.A.
Copyright © 1999 by Stephen T. Sinatra, M.D., F.A.C.C.
Printed and bound in the United States of America
International Standard Book Number: 0-87983-808-6
09 10 RCP 20 19 18 17 16

Contents

INTRODUCTION

Coenzyme Q10 first came to my attention in 1982 when I read a journal article[1] reporting on its effectiveness in helping patients come off heart-lung bypass, a transition from surgery that is fraught with danger. I was intrigued, so I clipped the article. However, like most of my colleagues at that time in my professional growth and development, I still had some bias against simple nonpharmaceutical compounds, vitamins and cofactors. I failed to appreciate that their effects could be so dramatic.

It took me four years to become convinced enough to let go of my rigid conventional medical thinking; in 1986 I began to integrate CoQ10 into my cardiology practice. I was highly impressed with the results and soon became committed to spreading the word about this remarkable compound. In the last dozen years, I have recommended Coenzyme Q10 for thousands of patients in my medical practice and continue to recommend it to the thousands of subscribers who read *HeartSense*, my monthly newsletter.

My passion for CoQ10 today goes well beyond its use in clinical cardiology. CoQ10 is an important medicinal that can alleviate a much wider range of human suffering. Educating my medical colleagues and the general public about CoQ10 has become a mission for me. I have published papers on it in both the medical and lay literature and, with the assistance of pharmacists, chemists and other doctors, I have participated in double-blind research regarding the technological and scientific aspects of how CoQ10 is best absorbed by the body.

The body requires certain blood levels of CoQ10 to function properly and, when blood levels fall, an increased vulnerability to disease and premature aging occurs. It is my belief that supplemental CoQ10 not only improves the quality of life in patients with diseases, but also saves lives.

The purpose of this book is to increase public awareness of the profound clinical implications of this vital compound. It is my hope that this communication will deliver the CoQ10 story to as many people as possible.

CoQ10: A MIRACLE IN OUR MIDST

In October 1996 I had just returned from a conference in Florida when I got a call from a man who asked me to take his mother as a patient in transfer from another hospital. She was 79 years old and had been admitted to a community hospital in Connecticut with heart failure complicated by pneumonia. It was the first time she had ever been in the hospital in her entire life, except for childbirth. Previously, she was a healthy, vibrant woman.

She had been on a ventilator for three-and-a-half weeks, receiving powerful steroids and high concentrations of oxygen. Her days were numbered. Her son, a Ph.D. biochemist, was an expert in CoQ10 and other nutritional supplements. He asked the doctors at the community hospital if he could place his mother on CoQ10, but they refused. He then proceeded to bring in reams of research literature, but the doctors still wouldn't hear of it. He was very upset. He even went to the hospital administrators—they asked him to leave the hospital. Lawyers became involved. It was a disaster.

Because of their lack of knowledge and their fear and bias against nonconventional supplementation and because CoQ10 was not on formulary in the hospital, the doctors refused to consider this alternative treatment for the woman, and her concerned family was labeled "interfering." The physicians asked the family to end life support, but twice the daughter refused to "pull the plug."

When the son called me on the telephone, I was very direct. "I can't take your mother in transfer. They will have to bag-breathe her for over 40 minutes in an ambulance. She'll probably die." He was quick to reply. "At least with you she will have a fighting chance because, if she stays where she is, she's certainly going to die." I told him that if his mother was transferred in the ambulance, I could not be responsible. He was willing to take the chance, and she was transferred.

When I first saw Mary in the intensive care unit at Manchester Memorial Hospital, she was semicomatose, respirator-dependent, and responded only to verbal command and pain stimulation. Her pulmonary care was similar to that received at the previous hospital. The only change in her therapy was nutritional: 450 mg of Coenzyme Q10 was given through her feeding tube daily. Mary also received a multivitamin/mineral preparation that I had developed as well as one gram of magnesium intravenously on a daily basis. Although I had some hope for Mary, the other critical care doctors and nurses were extremely skeptical of using CoQ10 in this life-threatening case despite the fact that CoQ10 had been on formulary at our hospital for several years. What we were all about to observe was truly a resurrection.

On the third day, Mary started to come out of her coma. After 10 days, she was weaned off the ventilator. Four days later, sitting up in a wheelchair and using only supplemental oxygen, she was discharged to an extended care facility.

I have had the good fortune to see Mary in my office on several occasions since that time. She is enjoying a good quality of life on conventional medical therapy plus 360 mg of CoQ10 per day. When I last spoke with her family, she was reorganizing a vast library of about 3,000 books.

For me, Mary's story is not unusual. I have personally treated and heard of many anecdotal cases of people seemingly "left for dead" who have been similarly resurrected by the compound called Coenzyme Q10, which I believe is a proven miracle nutrient.

As a specialist, it is unthinkable for me to practice good cardiology without the help of Coenzyme Q10. And, for the thousands of people with cardiac conditions so severe that they need a heart transplant, CoQ10 may be a suitable alternative that not only enhances quality of life but extends survival as well. For some, it serves as a potent medicinal while for others it may literally buy time until a donor heart is available.

Research has shown that CoQ10 is an indisputable heart remedy, but most doctors have never even heard of it. And even those physicians who are aware of CoQ10 most likely dismiss it. Why is this so?

Although Coenzyme Q10 represents the greatest potential breakthrough for cardiovascular disease and some other illnesses as well, the resistance of the medical profession to using this essential nutrient represents one of the greatest potential tragedies in medicine.

As a cardiologist myself, I believe that Coenzyme Q10 is one of the greatest medicinal advances in the 20th century for the treatment of heart disease.

Hundreds of scientific studies and thousands of clinical applications have documented that this substance, which is produced by every living cell of the body, has proven benefits for treating a wide variety of clinical cardiac conditions including congestive heart failure, high blood pressure, angina ("heart cramp") and arrhythmia as well as other cardiological situations.

Yet, despite a large body of available information, a therapeutic description in a 1997 textbook of mainstream cardiology[1] and the fact that CoQ10 is used by many board-certified cardiologists in this country as well as in western Europe and Japan, the vitamin is still virtually ignored by the majority of clinical cardiologists and most of the conventional medical establishment as well.

Unfortunately, the many patients who are not helped by conventional treatments alone, but could be supported by the addition of Coenzyme Q10, will never even be given a chance to receive it. This was certainly true for my patient, Mary, before she was transferred to Manchester Memorial Hospital.

It is also tragic that, in addition to the widespread ignorance about nutritional medicine, there is also such negative bias against it. The rejection of Coenzyme Q10 as a potent, nonpharmacological treatment defies the imagination. It is apparently difficult for highly trained medical personnel, well-versed in pharmacology and technology, to believe that anything so simple and so natural can be as effective as the highly engineered drugs modern medicine has to offer. Most American cardiologists cannot acknowledge that a natural substance not manufactured by pharmaceutical industry giants, could be so valuable. All of these factors have rendered Coenzyme Q10 a victim of politics, bias, insufficient marketing, economics and ignorance of the results of real science.

Another blockade has been the patent issue. Since Coenzyme Q10 is not patentable, there is no economic incentive for major pharmacological companies to develop it as a product. Although pharmaceutical companies will usually encourage their sales representatives to start a campaign to educate physicians about new products, the distributors of Coenzyme Q10 do not have the financial and physical resources to "detail" CoQ10 as a major medicinal. Such an effort is just too costly for any company to take on when it cannot expect to have the exclusive patent or corner on the market.

Today, anyone can purchase any number of brands of Coenzyme Q10 in a health food store. Unfortunately, without massive physician education supported by ongoing research and pharmaceutical representation, Coenzyme Q10 will probably remain controversial until the evidence on the importance of this nutrient becomes so compelling that it will finally receive the respect it deserves.

Clinical research has demonstrated that serious Coenzyme Q10 deficiencies exist in our population due to a multitude of factors, including the fact that CoQ10 production gradually declines in the body with aging. CoQ10 supplementation has been shown to increase blood levels of this essential nutrient resulting in many clinical benefits.

The recovery of an ailing heart, such as in the case of Mary, is but a fraction of the entire CoQ10 story. This amazing nutrient is being used for a wide variety of serious degenerative diseases, including heart disease, high blood pressure, cancer, periodontal disease, diabetes, neurological disorders and even aging itself. In addition, Coenzyme Q10 is considered a medicinal for relieving male infertility and has the ability to support the immune system in the HIV/ AIDS syndrome. In fact, CoQ10 seems to support almost any tissue in need of assistance, repair or help.

HISTORY OF CoQ10

Like many other incredible breakthroughs in metabolic medicine, the discovery of Coenzyme Q10 was actually quite accidental. Postdoctoral students were performing experiments on beef heart mitochondria at the University of Wisconsin Laboratory in 1957 under the direction of Dr. D. Green when Dr. Fred L. Crane[1] noticed a frothy substance that consistently rose to the top of their test tubes. One day, out of curiosity, Dr. Crane scraped off some of the yellow crystalline substance and viewed it under his microscope. Unable to identify it, he sent a few milligrams to Dr. Karl Folkers, who reisolated it at the Merck, Sharpe and Dohme Laboratories in Rahway, N.J. Folkers determined its chemical structure to be 2,3 dimethoxy-5 methyl-6-decaprenyl-1, 4-benzoquinone.

In 1957, Dr. D.E. Wolf and his colleagues at the Merck Pharmaceutical Company reported on the chemical structure of this quinone. Q defines its membership in the quinone group, and the figure 10 identifies the number of isoprenoid units in its side chain. Dr. R.A. Morton[2] called the Q10 compound *ubiquinone* because of its widespread appearance in living organisms.

Dr. Folkers, leader of the Merck research group, became so intrigued that he proceeded to spearhead pioneer studies into the biochemistry, action and clinical aspects of this new discovery, now called as Coenzyme Q10. Merck, although sitting on the potential to investigate and develop Coenzyme Q10, dropped the ball at this point; thus it was the Japanese, in 1963, who began testing the supplement on humans on an individual case basis.

The first organized clinical trial of Coenzyme Q10 in human subjects was performed by Dr. Y. Yamamura and his col-

The History of CoQ10

1957................. CoQ10 first isolated from beef heart by Frederick Crane.

1958................. Karl Folkers at Merck, Sharpe & Dohme determines the precise chemical structure.

Mid-1960s........ Professor Yamamura of Japan is the first to use Coenzyme Q7 (related compound) in corgestive heart failure.

1972................. Dr. Littarru (Italy) and Dr. Folkers (U.S.) document a CoQ10 deficiency in human heart disease.

Mid-1970s........ Japanese perfect industrial technology of fermentation to produce pure CoQ10 in significant quantities.

1976................. CoQ10 is placed on formulary in Japanese hospitals.

1978................. Peter Mitchell receives Nobel Prize for CoQ10 and energy transfer.

1980s............... Enthusiasm for CoQ10 leads to tremendous increase in number and size of clinical studies around the world.

1985................. Dr. Per Langsjoen in Texas reports the profound impact CoQ10 has in cardiomyopathy in double-blind studies.

1990s............... Explosion of use of CoQ10 in health food industry.

1992................. CoQ10 placed on formulary at Manchester Memorial Hospital, Manchester, Connecticut.

1996................. 9th international conference on CoQ10 in Ancona, Italy. Scientists and physicians report on a variety of medical conditions improved by CoQ10 administration. Blood levels of at least 2.5 ug/ml and preferably higher required for most medicinal purposes.

1996–97........... Gel-Tec, a division of Tishcon Corp., under the leadership of Raj Chopra, develops the "Biosolv process," allowing for greater bioavailability of supplemental CoQ10 in the body.

1997................. CoQ10 hits textbooks of mainstream cardiology.

leagues at Osaka University in 1965, where the nutrient was given to patients with heart disease. In 1971, Drs. Folkers (USA) and Littarru (Italy) reported that the patients with periodontal disease were often deficient in Coenzyme Q10, and one year later they demonstrated a deficiency of CoQ10 in cases of human heart disease.[3]

In 1973, Dr. Folkers completed a double-blind study with Dr. Matsumura (Japan), employing CoQ10 for gum disease, and reported it as superior to the current treatment for periodontal diseases. Not long afterward, Dr. E.G. Wilkinson, prominent U.S. Air Force periodontal specialist, confirmed that not only did he too find CoQ10 deficiencies in patients with gum disease, but that oral doses of the supplement promoted healing.

It was not until 1974 that large enough quantities of CoQ10 could be harvested to support organized clinical trials in large groups of people. Scientists in Japan perfected the industrial technology to produce pure CoQ10 in sufficient quantities for distribution. So it was at this crossroads that CoQ10 gained widespread acceptance in Japan and became more available for those with heart disease.

Meanwhile, one night, at about 3:00 a.m., English scientist Peter Mitchell was struggling to sleep. Looking at an incomplete schema in his mind's eye, he suddenly had an "Aha!" experience and realized the solution to a complicated puzzle he had been trying to piece together. Subsequently, in 1978 he was given the Nobel Prize for hypothesizing how CoQ10 works and describing energy transfer processes within the mitochondria of the cell.[4] The momentum continued to build in the latter half of the 1970s.

By 1982, CoQ10 had reached a level of consumption in Japan that rivaled that country's top five medications. It has been Japanese, and later European scientists and physicians who have conducted the majority of clinical trials employing CoQ10. In a 1985 review article, Dr. Yamamura[5] listed 67 clinical studies that evaluated CoQ10 in cases of heart muscle disease, arrhythmias and heart damage from drugs, high blood pressure and stroke. At the same time, Per Langsjoen, M.D. in Texas, testing CoQ10 in double-blind fashion, reported on CoQ10 as a valuable nutrient for cardio-myopathy.[6]

Just one year later (1986), the prestigious Priestley Medal of the American Chemical Society was awarded to Dr. Folkers, often called the "father of CoQ10," for his research into this nutrient as well as others. At about the same time, Lars Ernster of Sweden expanded on Coenzyme Q10's significance as a free radical scavenger.[7]

In the 1990s, Coenzyme Q10 became a top-selling supplement in health food stores, where consumers, reading about its healing potential for so many medical problems, began buying it for themselves. Today, the Internet is crowded with CoQ10 wholesalers and those who just want a billboard on which to place their latest CoQ10 success story.

As of 1997 there have been over 100 observational, epidemiological and population studies on Coenzyme Q10, and currently there are at least 19 placebo-controlled trials,* 16 showing benefits and 3 reporting no significant therapeutic responses. Two of the studies that showed no benefit were conducted by the same group of authors who failed to include research design blood levels of CoQ10 before and after treatment. Even the authors of these negative studies admit that plasma levels should be measured to demonstrate sufficient absorption of CoQ10.

From 1976 through 1996 there have been nine international symposia on the biochemical and clinical aspects of Coenzyme Q10. These symposia alone have compiled over 350 papers, presented by over 200 different physicians and scientists from 18 different countries who have investigated Coenzyme Q10 supplementation in a wide range of medical disorders.*

But, in spite of all this published research, very few American physicians have heard of CoQ10, know how it works or recommend it to those patients whom it would benefit. Those who could guide the public best about when and how to use CoQ10, are ignorant of and disinter-

*For a complete list of these references, contact Keats Publishing, Inc., Box 876, New Canaan, CT 06840.

ested in it. The research scientists seem to be the only ones in the U.S. who understand the incredible healing capacity of CoQ10, and they continue to struggle to get the word out to physicians.

DEFINITION AND BIOCHEMISTRY OF CoQ10

Coenzyme Q10, or ubiquinone, is a vitamin-like substance that is found in virtually all cells of the human body. Naturally found in foods, the usual average daily dietary intake is 2 to 5 mg per day. However, the amount received from dietary sources is insufficient to produce any substantial clinical effects, especially in those with pathological situations such as periodontal disease, high blood pressure, heart disease, impaired immunity and so on. Although some Coenzyme Q10 is present in most plant and animal cells, it is found in larger concentrations in beef heart, pork, sardines, anchovies, mackerel, salmon, broccoli, spinach and nuts. Coenzyme Q10 is also synthesized in all tissues of the body.

The biosynthesis of CoQ10, which is the dominant source in man, involves a complex process requiring the amino acid tyrosine and at least eight vitamins and several trace elements. The quinone ring of Coenzyme Q10 is synthesized from tyrosine. The polyisoprenoid side chain is formed from acetyl CoA. Thus, the structure of Coenzyme Q10 includes a benzoquinone or chemical compound containing a six-carbon benzene ring which features two sets of double-bonded carbons. The isoprenoid side chain is attached at the sixth carbon on the ring.[1] The number of isoprene units varies from 0 to 10, depending upon the animal species. In humans, Coenzyme Q10 has 10 isoprene units—thus the name Coenzyme Q10.

Biochemical Structure of Coenzyme Q10

Coenzyme Q_{10}

A deficiency in any of the required amino acids, vitamins and other minerals impairs the endogenous formation of CoQ10 in the body. Without CoQ10, our body cannot survive. As CoQ10 levels in the cells fall, so does our general health. What is CoQ10, and why is it so important and crucial for survival?

CoQ10, as a fat-soluble compound, functions as a coenzyme in the energy-producing metabolic pathways of every cell of the body with a powerful antioxidant activity.

As an antioxidant, the reduced form of Coenzyme Q10 inhibits lipid peroxidation (oxidation of fats) in both cell membranes and serum low-density lipoproteins (LDL) and also protects proteins and DNA from oxidative damage. Coenzyme Q10 also plays a vital role in combating free radical stress.[2]

FREE RADICALS AND DISEASE

While we cannot see the effects of oxidation (free radical damage) in our body, we are all familiar with common examples of oxidation in the world around us, like the browning of a freshly cut apple or the rusting of metal. Oxidation results from the breakdown of oxygen molecules as they combine with other molecules in our body. Such oxidation can be the result of the body's normal metabolism of the foods we eat, or it can occur in the body as a result of external forces such as radiation, air pollution, alcohol or heavy metal intoxication, use of pharmaceutical and over-the-counter drugs, infections or even strenuous exercise. Under any of these circumstances, excessive free radical stress occurs.

Free radicals are highly reactive molecules produced during oxidation. Interfering with enzymatic reactions, free radicals do their damage by attacking cells in the body. Because these bombarding molecules have unpaired electrons, they collide like unguided missiles, causing disruptions of cells, membranes and even DNA itself. The body struggles to defend itself, engaging in a continuous biochemical battle between the invading toxins (rancid fats, heavy metals, cigarette smoke, etc.) and the immune system.

During this molecular warfare, the toxic waste of combat begins to accumulate in the body, producing an enormous metabolic stress which, over time, can lead to disease.

During free radical stress, the oxidants act like invaders, taking away electrons from precious molecules. The antioxidants that we naturally produce in the body or which we add to our diet, such as in foods or supplements rich in vitamins C, E and the minerals selenium and zinc, help to cancel out the chemical activity of free radicals and protect our cells. Like suicide pilots who sacrifice themselves for the benefit of their cause, antioxidants surrender electrons easily in these metabolic reactions and function to neutralize the invading oxidants.

Since the antioxidant activity of CoQ10 is directly related to energy carrier function, CoQ10 molecules can generally undergo oxidation/reduction. As CoQ10 accepts electrons it becomes reduced, and as it gives up electrons it becomes oxidized. In the reduced form, Coenzyme Q10 can give up electrons quickly and easily and thus act as a powerful antioxidant against free radicals.[3] Since free radicals contain highly reactive molecules with unpaired electrons, CoQ10's remarkable donor activity makes it an ideal antioxidant. Acting like a bodyguard, Q10's actions protect the body.

Coenzyme Q10, like other antioxidants, can engulf free radicals before they do their damage, protecting DNA, cellular membranes and even various enzyme systems involved in the metabolism of food and oxygen in the body. We know that the health of every cell in the body depends upon the balance of free radicals and antioxidants. It has been theorized that such antioxidant activity has been needed for millions of years, ever since oxygen appeared in the earth's atmosphere.

Although oxygen is necessary for aerobic life, the breakdown (metabolism) of oxygen has metabolic consequences. Free radicals, the oxidant byproducts of normal metabolism, are causative agents of the degenerative diseases of the 20th century, such as cancer and heart disease, and also culprits in aging itself.

But not all free radicals are bad. Free radicals also play a key role in normal biological functions that support necessary life processes such as mitochondrial respiration,[4] platelet activation,[5] and prostaglandin synthesis.[6] Thus, free radicals have a dark side and a bright side. This paradox of free radical chemistry has generated tremendous interest in the health-care profession, especially for those interested in aging and preventive medicine.

Since the electron-rich reduced form of Coenzyme Q10, vitamin E and other antioxidants support antioxidant defenses, their presence becomes vital in strategies to prevent free radical damage and premature aging. The antioxidant activity of CoQ10 is especially noteworthy in other areas as well. Because the oxidized form of vitamin E can be reduced by Coenzyme Q10, vitamin E regeneration is enhanced. As a recycler of vitamin E, CoQ10 makes its antioxidant partner more available to help trap free radicals before they do their damage.

Scientific research has demonstrated that a combination supplementation of vitamin E and CoQ10 makes LDL more resistant to oxidation than when vitamin E is used alone.[7,8] Because the oxidation of LDL is the pivotal step in the cause of atherosclerosis, this finding has major implications in the prevention of coronary heart disease.

It is also important to note the membrane stabilizing activity of CoQ10 and its very recently discovered favorable effects on platelets[9] and platelet function. All of these properties of CoQ10 enhance its anti-aging benefits.

ENERGY AND ATP

CoQ10's bioenergetic activity is probably its most important function. The term "bioenergetic" is used in the field of biochemistry to describe compounds that support cellular energy. Such energy enhancement occurs in the mitochondria (the powerful furnaces that generate energy in cells). It is there, in the so-called cellular boiler room, that Coenzyme Q10 acts as an essential component in the electron transport chain where metabolic energy is released. It is the generation of this chemical energy that supplies the vital force so necessary for life.

The healthy operation of the human energy system requires the adequate formation of energy. This process is dependent upon a sufficient intake of oxygen and essential nutrients, vitamins and cofactors. The end product is the pulsation of healthy cells. Every living cell has pulsatory activity. The cells have resting as well as generative phases. The maintenance of proper cellular functioning depends upon a multitude of complex variables.

A deficiency or an imbalance in any part of the system may contribute, over time, to the impaired functioning of cells, tissues, organs and eventually the entire body. We need to view the concept of energy as both quantitative and qualitative. A proper balance of oxygen and nutritional components, such as vitamins, minerals, enzymes and cofactors, is required on a second-to-second basis for the cells to function optimally. It is this total concept of energy that demonstrates that Coenzyme Q10 is an essential component to maintain the energetic vital life force.

CoQ10 is involved in the reactions of at least three mitochondrial enzymes, rendering it the essential component of the electron transport chain. In a series of complex reactions involving pathways in the mitochondrial chain, the synthesis of adenosine triphosphate (ATP) occurs.[10]

ATP is a high-energy phosphate compound necessary to fuel all cellular functions. Think of ATP as a "high octane fuel" used for all the energetic transactions in the body. We may think that we eat only to satisfy hunger or our taste buds or to socialize. But the truth is we consume food to get the energy sources required to generate ATP, the body's major form of stored energy that ultimately drives the machinery of our bodies.

All cellular function depends on an adequate supply of ATP. ATP facilitates the chemical energy released by oxidation and other cellular reactions, maintaining the essential and the diverse functions of life. CoQ10's role as a mobile electron carrier in the mitochondrial electron transfer chain makes it the pivotal nutrient for the production of cellular energy. In biochemical terms, Coenzyme Q10 supports every cell in the human body by preventing the depletion of the precursors necessary for ATP production. It is this key bioenergetic property that makes Coenzyme Q10 so unique. In simple language, Coenzyme Q10 provides the spark in the mitochondria of each cell to initiate the energy process. This is why CoQ10 is vital for life itself.

Think of the body as a fine-tuned car. Functioning on low levels of Coenzyme Q10 would be similar to running a car on a low-octane fuel. With such poor octane energy fuel, the cylinders in the car's high-performance engine (where the gasoline is ignited) would not have sufficient force to move the pistons evenly. The energy that then drives the car would be inadequate, resulting in misfiring pistons and sluggish, undependable movement. Similarly, the human body must have high-octane fuel to create the energy to carry on the basic processes of life, such as respiration and the breakdown and assimilation of foods. And for more complex operations, such as the pulsation of the heart, walking, mental activity, playing golf and so forth, there is an even higher demand for energy. But where does this energy come from?

All the energy production in the body is the result of this complicated biochemical process, starting with the oxidative phosphorylation pathways in which ATP is formed. So without Coenzyme Q10, there would be no "spark" in the mitochondria to ignite this energy transfer. Without energy-rich compounds of ATP, the body would stall and cease to function.

In essence, without adequate energy the cells would be inefficient, lackluster, and be vulnerable to free radical attack and disease. When a deficiency of Coenzyme Q10 exists, the cellular "engines" misfire and, over time, they may eventually fail or even die. The bioenergetics of a failing heart or a failing immune system will inevitably lead to the weakening of all the natural defenses against disease and premature aging.

HOW AND WHEN TO SUPPLEMENT WITH CoQ10

WHY DO DEFICIENCIES OCCUR?

As stated earlier, the body's manufacture of CoQ10 is a complex process that takes place in all cells, especially in the liver, and requires multiple vitamins, cofactors and amino acids. A deficiency in any of these components is very likely to impair the cell's ability to make CoQ10.

For example, if the body is deficient in folate, vitamins C, B12, B6, pantothenic acid and trace elements, to mention a few essential nutrients, the synthesis of CoQ10 could be significantly blocked. In addition, decreased dietary intake, chronic malnutrition or chronic disease can result in CoQ10 deficiencies.

In one clinical study of hospitalized patients on total intravenous nutrition without vitamin support, blood levels of CoQ10 plummeted 50 percent in just one week.[1] It has also been observed in both animal and human studies that aging is also associated with a decline in CoQ10 levels.[2]

Moreover, environmental stressors as well as lifestyle factors may reduce CoQ10 in body tissues. One lifestyle stressor is chronic high-intensity exercise. When athletes have been studied, lower blood levels of CoQ10 have been observed, most probably the result of the increased metabolic demands of chronically exercising muscles, resulting in an excess of free radicals.[3]

Other environmental factors that may result in CoQ10 deficiencies include cholesterol-lowering drugs such as the HMG-CoA reductase inhibitors.[4] Statin-like drugs, such as Lovastatin, Simvastatin, Pravastatin, to mention a few, often used to treat patients with high cholesterol levels are in this category of pharmaceuticals.

The population being treated with these HMG CoA reductase inhibitors to lower serum cholesterol is also at risk for CoQ10 depletion. Cholesterol production, as well as endogenous pathways for CoQ10 production, are both compromised by these drugs.

BIOSYNTHETIC PATHWAY OF CHOLESTEROL

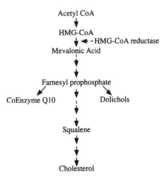

The enzyme 3-hydroxy-e-methylglutaryl Coenzyme A (HMG-CoA) reductase is necessary for the conversion of HMG-CoA to mevalonic acid, an early step in biosynthesis of cholesterol. Because mevalonic acid is also a precursor of Coenzyme Q10 via a branch of the cholesterol biosynthetic pathway, HMG-CoA reductase inhibitors could reduce serum concentrations of Coenzyme Q10.

It is extremely important that physicians be aware of the potential for statins to adversely affect CoQ10 levels. This effect certainly has major implications and ramifications for patients with cardiac disease. It is especially crucial that patients with congestive heart failure or an overactive thyroid be given additional supplemental doses of CoQ10 to offset the depleting effects of these cholesterol-reducing agents.

Moreover, when considering the free radical oxidation mechanism in arteriosclerosis, a decline in CoQ10 reserves may also adversely affect the course of arteriosclerosis *despite* optimal reduction of LDL cholesterol. Certainly, the adverse metabolic effect of these drugs requires further investigation.[5]

Perhaps the greatest source of CoQ10 deficiencies appears in tissues that are metabolically active, such as those found in the heart,[6,7] immune system, gingiva and an overactive thyroid gland.[8]

An overactive thyroid or even a pulsating heart, for that matter, requires additional Coenzyme Q10 support. Although Coenzyme Q10 is found in relatively high concentrations in the liver, the kidney and the lung, the heart requires the highest levels of ATP activity[9] because it is continually aerobic. Coenzyme Q10 support is essential for the healthy heart and critical for the failing one.

Tissue deficiencies and low serum blood levels of CoQ10 have been reported across a wide range of cardiovascular diseases, including congestive heart failure,[6,7] hypertension,[10] aortic valvular disease[11] and coronary artery disease.[12]

In summary, Coenzyme Q10 deficiencies may occur in several situations as a result of insufficient dietary intake, impairment in CoQ10 synthesis, environmental factors, excessive utilization by tissues or a combination of any of these factors. The profound effects of CoQ10 deficiency have stimulated clinical research into the role of exogenous supplementation as an appropriate therapeutic intervention.

Animal studies have shown that CoQ10 supplementation increases both tissue levels and mitochondrial levels of CoQ10.[13] Human experimental and clinical data have also provided extensive evidence that CoQ10 supplementation can increase blood levels in those with severe heart disease. So we know that it is possible to correct CoQ10 deficiencies by oral supplementation.

However, it is important to look at issues of therapeutic bioavailability and absorption of CoQ10 whenever we consider employing this nutrient. The case of a patient with refractory heart failure follows. For this woman, the CoQ10 dose made all the difference. Ultimately she was successfully managed as a result of an "error" in dosage that for her made the difference between life and death.

A CASE OF SEVERE CONGESTIVE HEART FAILURE

When she was 60 years of age, L.G. first developed symptoms of congestive heart failure (CHF), a condition in which the heart becomes congested with blood and is dangerously weakened.

L.G.'s heart failure began with a longstanding high blood pressure which had weakened her left ventricle. By age 67 she was congested by the fluid in her lungs (pulmonary edema), and her ejection fraction (EF—the percentage of blood pumped from the left ventricle with each heart beat) was reduced to 35 percent. The normal range is 50–70 percent. After a second episode of pulmonary edema, L.G. agreed to cardiac catheterization (angiogram), which showed an enlarged, stretched and weakened left ventricle and normal coronary arteries. She was treated with the usual pharmacological drugs for CHF.

Although L.G.'s quality of life was generally satisfactory, she suffered from intermittent bouts of CHF, and her health progressively went downhill. By the time I met her, L.G. was almost 80 years old and struggling for every breath.

It was October 1994, and L.G. weighed only 77 pounds and was suffering from severe weakness and weight loss, (end-stage cardiac cachexia). The echocardiogram showed a "leaky valve" and an EF of only 15 percent, barely enough to support a bed-to-chair lifestyle. I decided to prescribe 30 mg of CoQ10 three times a day (90 mg/day), my comfortable dosing level at that time. Despite the addition of this alternative therapy, L.G. developed marked edema, ascites (a collection of fluids in body cavities, especially the abdomen) and severe fatigue. Her breathing became so labored that she required two lung taps to withdraw the excess fluid from her chest. L.G. remained homebound. She was slowly dying.

I shared L.G.'s great disappointment in the face of her terminal situation, but then a miracle happened. L.G. accidentally started taking 300 mg of CoQ10 daily—more than triple the dose she had become accustomed to taking! Her son had mistakenly purchased 100 mg capsules instead of the usual 30 mg supplements. Four weeks later, L.G. experienced a steady and marked improvement, so I continued her on the 300 mg dose.

Three months later she became more active and mobile. A repeat echocardiogram proved that her ejection fraction had risen from about 15 percent to 20 percent (a ⅓ increase). In addition, the ultrasound of her heart demonstrated a reduction in her valve leakage.

A full year after she began taking CoQ10 supplements, and eight months after I maintained her on a dosage of 300 mg daily, L.G. was shopping and visiting relatives. She became so active, in fact, that she fell down and fractured her hip! Previously considered a high surgical risk, L.G. underwent a successful hip replacement operation. On 300 mg of CoQ10 daily, her blood level was 4.8 ug/ml, an ideal blood level for her severe cardiac condition.

SUPPLEMENTATION WITH CoQ10

What can we learn from L.G.'s case? First of all, research indicates that if levels of CoQ10 decline by 25 percent, our organs may become deficient and impaired. When levels decline by 75 percent, serious tissue damage and even death may occur.[14,15] It has also been determined by advanced blood level technology, that heart tissue levels of CoQ10 are lower in cases of advanced congestive heart failure. Since myocardial tissue levels of CoQ10 may be restored significantly by oral supplementation, the use of Coenzyme Q10 therapy should be the first defense against congestive heart failure. How much CoQ10 is needed?

Although the cardiovascular literature is filled with multiple studies showing the positive effects of CoQ10 supplements for cardiac patients, the usual recommended dosage is still only 90 mg to 150 mg daily. But, as the case of L.G. clearly teaches us, many patients simply do not respond to such minimal doses. When I have critically ill patients like L.G., I ask myself three questions when considering the CoQ10 dose:

1. Is the dose sufficient to raise the patient's blood level of CoQ10?
2. Does the CoQ10 preparation the patient is taking actually deliver the amount of CoQ10 that is stated on the bottle?
3. How do I know the patient's level of CoQ10 without drawing blood levels?

An adequate dose of CoQ10 will usually result in symptom improvement. If there is a lack of response to a low dose of CoQ10, a higher dose may be indicated. Certainly this was the case for L.G., who required high supplemental doses of CoQ10 to attain a significant blood level with a therapeutic effect.

I have learned one key thing from many patients like L.G.: if the initial response to low doses of CoQ10 is poor, we need not give up. Instead we need to be more aggressive, increase the dosage and maintain it over time. With this aggressive approach, more patients can recapture their quality of life. It is the sickest patients, with the most compromised quality of life, who stand to gain the most from high doses of CoQ10.

This brings me to the second lesson I have recently learned: not all CoQ10 preparations are the same, because some CoQ10 preparations are less bioavailable than others.

By that I mean that CoQ10 is not as readily absorbed by the body, due to a multitude of factors. You can be receiving far less strength than the label indicates, and failure to improve may be proof of that.

For example, I have encountered many patients who came to me taking large doses of CoQ10 without a significant therapeutic effect. After drawing blood levels on these individuals, I was shocked to find low blood levels despite the fact that many of these people were taking 200 to 400 mg of CoQ10 daily. This can indicate one of two things.

First, the patient may not have responded to CoQ10 because he or she cannot absorb it. Secondly, the product may be at fault. If the patient does not respond to high doses of CoQ10, the product he or she is taking may not contain enough pure CoQ10 or the product may lack bioavailability because of compounds or fillers in the preparation.

Because adequate blood levels and bioavailability are the key to treating very sick people, I participated in two small double-blind studies that evaluated the bioavailability of several different CoQ10 preparations.[16,17]

CoQ10 Blood Level Research

Commercially available CoQ10 supplements are usually oil-based suspensions in soft-gel capsules, cap-tabs or powder-filled hard-shelled capsules, the former being the most common. While there have been many clinical studies using these preparations, there are very few reports, both in animal models and human subjects in the literature, comparing the absorption or the bioavailability of the CoQ10 in these products.

There are many CoQ10 supplements available commercially, but they are not equally bioavailable. As a fat-soluble compound, CoQ10 is poorly absorbed in water. It follows the same pathway as do other fats that are absorbed by the body. The breakdown of fat substances requires emulsification in the intestine (with the help of bile salts)) and the formation of micelles prior to absorption. Among the other factors affecting the absorption of exogenously administered CoQ10 are its particle size, degree of solubility and the type of food that is ingested with the supplement.

Although CoQ10 is classified as a lipid-soluble substance, its degree of solubility is extremely limited. Commercially available CoQ10 capsules contain either oil-based suspensions (softgels) or dry powder blends. When tested in the laboratory, many of these products show a total lack of dissolution, indicating that their bioavailability is negligible and they will be poorly absorbed.

In two separate studies[16,17], we compared the relative bioavailability of CoQ10 in commercially available products, i.e., an oil suspension in softgel, powder-filled hard-shelled capsules, a tablet formula, and Q-Gel, a new solubilized CoQ10 formula in a softgel (using the new biosolv process).

These two studies, each involving 24 healthy volunteers, demonstrated that the bioavailability of CoQ10 can be greatly enhanced by using appropriate solubilization techniques. The following graphs reflect clinical studies which demonstrate the higher blood levels of Q-gel over standard CoQ10 preparations overtime.

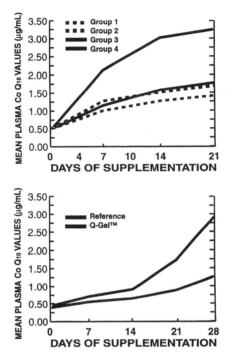

With Q-Gel, plasma CoQ10 values showed a sharp increase, reaching a therapeutic range above 2.5 ug/ml within three to four weeks with further increases over time.

Although the optimal dose of CoQ10 is not known for every pathological situation, researchers agree that levels of 2.5 ug/ml and preferably 3.5 ug/ml[18, 19] are required to have a positive impact on severely diseased hearts. Therefore, whenever employing CoQ10 as a supplement, it is important to note not only the amount being taken, but also how it is absorbed and delivered to the body.

Product bioavailability is obviously a major concern to consumers. All CoQ10 is made in Japan and sold to various companies, but the packaging and preparations differ. New research shows that the delivery of CoQ10 in softsules, which are both water- and fat-soluble, is superior to the dry form; more CoQ10 gets into the bloodstream.

Keeping delivery in mind, what dose of CoQ10 should one take? Whether taking capsules, cap-tabs or regular oil-based CoQ10, my recommendations are as follows:

- **30 to 100 mg daily** as a preventive in cardiovascular or periodontal disease and for patients taking Hmg-CoA reductase inhibitors.
- **90 to 180 mg daily** for the treatment of angina pectoris, cardiac arrhythmia, high blood pressure and moderate gingival disease.
- **180 to 360 mg daily** for congestive heart failure and dilated cardiomyopathy.

Note: For a severely impaired immune system, as in cancer, even higher doses of CoQ10 may be required.

Once a therapeutic effect is obtained, that is, there is improved well-being, lowered blood pressure, improved shortness of breath, better gum tissues, and so on, the maintenance dose may be adjusted. Fifteen mg of Q-Gel softsule is the equivalent of approximately 50 mg of standard CoQ10.

I have observed that for many cardiac conditions, especially CHF and cardiomyopathy, the therapeutic dose must be the maintenance dose or symptoms will return. I have noted that some patients, well-maintained on CoQ10, will have a return of symptoms if they change the brand or the dosage they are taking. Obviously, they may be getting a poorer delivery system, but if the situation is not remedied, their cardiac symptoms may return and the cause may not be recognized. Stopping or reducing CoQ10 is similar to altering intake of cardiac drugs such as beta blockers. Relapses can certainly occur.

For those using CoQ10 as adjunct therapy in treating a serious illness, it may be appropriate to ask the doctor to have a blood level obtained since blood levels are the most accurate assessment of how CoQ10 is being absorbed and delivered to tissues and organs. When CoQ10 is delivered in sufficient dosage, it will support the tissues in need.

COENZYME Q10 IN CLINICAL CARDIOVASCULAR DISEASE

A deficiency of Coenzyme Q10 is quite common in cardiac patients. This has been well-documented in myocardial biopsies, especially in patients undergoing cardiac transplantation.[1] Researchers found the lowest tissue levels of CoQ10 in the sickest and most compromised patients. Most of them were, in fact, what we call class IV cardiac patients, those who have symptoms—such as extreme fatigue, chest discomfort or shortness of breath—even when they are just resting.

Because the heart is so metabolically active and requires a constant supply of ATP for continued pulsation, it is especially vulnerable to CoQ10 deficiencies. Fortunately, however, the heart muscle is also the most responsive tissue in the body to CoQ10 supplementation, rendering CoQ10 a nutrient with great promise for the treatment of cardiovascular disease.

CoQ10 deficiencies have been confirmed among patients with congestive heart failure, coronary artery disease, angina pectoris, cardiomyopathy, hypertension, mitral valve prolapse, as well as among those who have had coronary artery bypass surgery. In fact, the literature so well documents both CoQ10 deficiencies and response to supplementation for heart disease that in 1992 I asked the chief of pharmacy in the hospital where I practice to place CoQ10 on hospital formulary.

Coenzyme Q10 can be administered in a wide variety of clinical settings for cardiovascular disease:

1. Angina pectoris
2. Unstable anginal syndrome

3. Myocardial preserving agent during mechanical or pharmacological thrombolysis
4. Myocardial preserving agent for cardiac surgery
5. Congestive heart failure, diastolic dysfunction
6. Toxin-induced cardiotoxicity (i.e., a side effect of adriamycin)
7. Essential and renovascular hypertension
8. Ventricular arrhythmia
9. Mitral valve prolapse
10. To prevent oxidation of LDL

Although clinical research has consistently shown Coenzyme Q10 to be clinically effective for coronary artery disease,[2-4] arrhythmia,[5] high blood pressure,[6,7] as well as the cardiotoxic side effects of adriamycin treatment[8,9] (a form of chemotherapy), over the past two decades many clinical investigations into Coenzyme Q10 have focused on congestive heart failure and cardiomyopathy.[10-17]

A strong correlation between low blood and tissue levels of Coenzyme Q10 and the severity of heart failure has been consistently confirmed.[1, 18-20] Experimental and clinical data have provided extensive evidence that CoQ10 supplementation in patients with cardiomyopathy and congestive heart failure has resulted in improvements of multiple indicators of the heart's pumping ability, including left ventricular function, ejection fraction, exercise tolerance, diastolic dysfunction, clinical outcome and quality of life.[10-17]

CONGESTIVE HEART FAILURE

The management of congestive heart failure (CHF) and dilated cardiomyopathy (often end-stage CHF) are perhaps the most difficult challenges faced by most cardiologists today. In fact, as a practicing cardiologist for over 20 years, I have often found the medication juggling act in recycling bouts of CHF to be among my worst treatment nightmares. Although there are excellent conventional approaches in the battle against CHF, the fact remains that many patients do not fully respond to even the most high-powered drugs, and some cannot tolerate the many side effects that often occur as a result of employing them. Despite modern medicine and technology, the quality of life for those with a weakened heart muscle and chronic CHF is compromised, and their very survival often remains guarded. I have found, however, that many of these individuals do improve when I combine conventional approaches (such as diuretics and digitalis) with complementary approaches, such as CoQ10 treatment.

Remember, the cardiovascular benefits of CoEnzyme Q10 are due primarily to its ability to do the following:

- Directly support ATP (energy production) in the mitochondria of the cell
- Act as a potent antioxidant
- Stabilize cell membranes
- Reduce platelet size, distribution and stickiness, limiting platelet activity

All of these actions are especially important for people who suffer congestive heart failure for which low energy output, free radical stress, cardiac arrhythmias, and enhanced clotting are common side effects. Actually, CHF is one of the main indications for the therapeutic administration of Coenzyme Q10. While it is beyond the scope of this book to discuss all of the literature concerning Coenzyme Q10 and congestive heart failure, I will review for you some of the most impressive studies. I will also define CHF and cardiomyopathy as well as comment on the crucial evaluations to keep in mind when making decisions about CoQ10 dosage.

CHF and dilated cardiomyopathy are conditions in which heart muscle is so weak it cannot effectively pump blood to the various areas of the body. Patients with this condition usually experience fatigue and shortness of breath with minimal exertion. Fluid buildup in the lower legs and congestion in the lungs may also occur. This is because the pumping ability of the heart depends upon the functional capacity of myocardial cells to expand and contract. In congestive heart failure, there are insufficient myocardial contractive forces in the heart muscle. In other words, the heart is not strong enough to pump blood out of the heart, which is why it becomes congested. The heart struggling with CHF is literally an exhausted starved heart with insufficient energy for the heart to pump.

The most common cause of congestive heart failure is coronary artery disease and the blockage of the heart arteries which can result in heart attacks. Longstanding high blood pressure, toxic drugs, alcohol abuse, valvular disease and various viral illnesses can also cause congestive heart failure.

Although the medical literature is replete with multiple studies showing the efficacy of Coenzyme Q10 for congestive heart failure, the evaluated dose-response relationships for CoQ10 have been evaluated within a narrow dose range. The majority of clinical studies have investigated the therapeutic effects of Coenzyme Q10 in doses ranging from 90 to 150 mg daily. At such doses, some patients have responded, while others have not.

For example, a study published in the 1990 *American Journal of Cardiology* (AJC),[21] a prestigious journal for heart specialists, reported that CoQ10 administration was associated with an increase in CoQ10 blood levels, indicating absorption of the nutrient. A corresponding improvement in heart function was documented by the researchers. Treated subjects also reported an enhanced quality of life. When we look at the results more closely, however, they suggest that clinical improvement may be a function of several variables, including individual dose effects.

The "response window"—the dose at which individuals will best appreciate clinical benefits from CoQ10 treatment—is highly variable, and often the sickest patients are so depleted that they require the highest dose levels of this nutrient.

Another double-blind, placebo-controlled crossover design study was conducted with 80 patients[11] and presented at the American Heart Association meeting in 1991. The reported improvements when CoQ10 was used as an adjunct to traditional therapy confirmed significant enhancement of exercise capacity and quality of life when compared to conventional drug therapy alone. This study, like the one previously discussed, shows the complementary support CoQ10 affords when added to conventional medical treatments.

A larger, double-blind trial was performed with 641 patients receiving placebo or CoQ10 in a dose of 2 mg/kg for one year. Investigators[12] reported a 50 percent reduction in pulmonary edema and a 20 percent reduction in hospitalization for the CoQ10 group compared to the placebo group. Perhaps the largest study to date demonstrating the efficacy and safety of CoQ10 for the treatment of congestive heart failure is the Italian multi-center trial by Baggio, et al,[17] that involved 2,664 patients with heart failure. In this study, the daily dosage of CoQ10 was 50–150 mg for 90 days, with the majority of patients receiving 100 mg daily.

Following three months of administration of CoQ10, symptoms decreased as follows:

Edema (fluid retention) 79%
Pulmonary edema (lung congestion of fluid) 78%
Liver enlargement 49%
Venous congestion 72%
Shortness of breath 53%
Heart palpitations 75%

Improvements in at least three symptoms were noted for 54 percent of patients. This large study is also reflective of what I have observed in my clinical practice of cardiology. There is no doubt about it: CoQ10 supplementation in patients with CHF does alleviate symptoms and improve quality of life. Other investigations have also shown the positive impact CoQ10 has on diastolic dysfunction, another crucial factor in congestive heart failure.

How CoQ10 Supports the Failing Heart
When the heart pulsates, there are several basic components to evaluate. Let's look at three stages that involve the ventricular muscles themselves. What we call "systolic function" describes the stage when the lower chambers of the heart muscle contract, squeezing blood out to the arteries. This stage requires adequate ATP energy in the cells of the heart muscle and a competent muscle to respond and contract effectively. The systolic contraction (whose pressure gradient correlates with systolic blood pressure) empties most of the blood out of the heart chambers (about 50 to 70 percent). Then there is a brief moment of rest (usually less

than one-third of a second) before the heart refills with blood for the next contraction.

This "diastole" stage is dependent upon energy and the ability of the heart muscle to s-t-r-e-t-c-h out without sagging, fill and accommodate adequate blood volume (about 200–400 ml). This entire cycle occurs in most people at approximately 50 to 90 times a minute on average, depending on the individual and the activity or energy demand.

Diastolic dysfunction, an inability of the heart to stretch and fill, is an early sign of myocardial failure despite the presence of normal systolic function. Symptoms of fatigue, shortness of breath, atypical chest pain, arrhythmia and physical activity impairment may precede by years the development of congestive heart failure. It is usually found more often in women than in men and is observed most often in clinical conditions such as high blood pressure, mitral valve prolapse and various types of cardiomyopathy or heart muscle disease. Diastolic dysfunction, or stiffening of the heart muscle, is a major cause of congestive heart failure.

Since diastolic function requires a larger amount of cellular energy than systolic contraction, more energy is required to fill the heart than to empty it. This additional requirement of energy activity makes CoQ10 a logical intervention. In a study of 109 patients with hypertensive heart disease and isolated diastolic dysfunction,[22] CoQ10 replacement resulted in clinical improvement, lowering of elevated blood pressure, improvement in diastolic function and a decrease in myocardial thickness in 53 percent of the hypertensives.

In another long-term study of 424 patients with systolic and/or diastolic dysfunction for over an eight-year period, an average 240 mg daily dose of Coenzyme Q10 resulted in blood levels greater than 2.0 per ug/ml.[23] These patients were followed for an average of 17.8 months with a total accumulation of 632 patient years.

It is interesting to note that medication requirements dropped for 43 percent of the participants, who were able to eliminate one to three conventional drugs. There were no side effects reported except for one case of nausea. This long-term study clearly demonstrated that Coenzyme Q10 is a safe and effective adjunct treatment for a broad range of cardiovascular disease, including congestive heart failure and dilated cardiomyopathy as well as for systolic and/or diastolic dysfunction in patients with hypertensive heart disease. This study also reemphasized the extreme importance of obtaining blood levels. When we know the actual blood level of CoQ10 for a given individual, we have a scientific basis from which to evaluate treatment effectiveness and clinical outcome.

The big question with CoQ10 remains, "What dose is necessary to affect symptoms?" And, if there is symptom alleviation at a particular dose level, how soon is it seen and what are the profiles of the responders? How do they differ from nonresponders? What are the factors that enhance or limit CoQ10 absorption? Are there other nutrients or factors that may either block or burn up CoQ10?

It was at the May 1996 International Conference on Coenzyme Q10, in Ancona, Italy, that I came to truly appreciate the importance of drawing serum levels of CoQ10 whenever possible. I learned that, first of all, not all CoQ10 preparations can be considered equal. Obviously, absorption and relative bioavailability can impact blood levels. Even if a CoQ10 product does have outstanding bioavailability, a low dosage of the nutrient may still result in a subtherapeutic serum level. By evaluating blood levels, we gain direct information on how to adjust CoQ10 dosing while evaluating clinical response.

Finding a laboratory that will perform CoQ10 levels is not always a feasible option for most practitioners. It requires special laboratory equipment and highly trained personnel, not available at most hospitals.

In general, I recommend that if any patient fails to respond to standard levels of CoQ10 intervention (i.e., 90 to 150 mg), it is essential to obtain a blood level for CoQ10. If a serum CoQ10 level is not feasible, then I would treat the patient clinically by doubling or even tripling the dose according to the patient's perceived symptoms, as cardiologists often do when dosing various drugs for treating CHF.

In conclusion, it is my belief that Coenzyme Q10 should be administered to any patient with congestive heart failure. This recommendation is also supported by a very recent meta-analysis. This analysis demonstrated a statistically significant improvement in ejection fraction and cardiac output, the two major physiological parameters of cardiac function.[24] Thus, an aggregate of eight double-blind studies published between 1984 and 1994 demonstrated that Coenzyme Q10 was effective in the treatment of congestive heart failure.

It is encouraging that researchers in Naples, Italy, projected from their findings that for every 1,000 cases of CHF treated with Coenzyme Q10 for one year, hospitalizations would be reduced by 20 percent.[12]

In this era of cost containment, this is indeed a compelling forecast. Moreover, the reduction in human suffering and cardiac dysfunction should also motivate physicians to consider CoQ10 as a first-line defense in CHF treatment, based on both the clinical research trials and the anecdotal case studies which I have presented.[25]

CARDIOMYOPATHY

Cardiomyopathy is a state in which the muscle tissue of the heart has become damaged, diseased, enlarged (hypertrophied) or stretched out and thinned (dilated), leaving the muscle fibers weakened. This most often happens as a result of scarring from heart attacks. Sometimes longstanding untreated high blood pressure may cause excess thickening of the left ventricle, rendering it a heavy, boggy and ineffective pump. Over time, such a chronic strain on the heart chambers may also result in a gradual weakening of the heart, resulting in thickening and stretching of the heart muscle, with subsequent ineffective myocardial contractions. This was certainly the case with L.G. (see page 25), who was afflicted with chronic high blood pressure.

Cardiomyopathy may be secondary to nutritional deficiencies, brought about by longstanding excess alcohol consumption or infection or secondary to severe inflammation such as a viral assault on the heart. The heart's enlarged silhouette may be detected on chest X-ray, while echocardiograms can bounce sound waves off the heart to determine chamber wall size, thickness and contractile ability.

Other causes of cardiomyopathy may be infiltration of the heart muscle with dense, rock-hard substances that may cause inefficient pulsation of the heart. One such condition is called amyloid heart disease. Infiltrating tumors may cause a similar situation.

Frequently, progressive, deteriorating, end-stage congestive heart failure is called a dilated cardiomyopathy when the chambers of the heart become so stretched and "baggy" that the pumping ability of the heart is impaired.

Cardiomyopathy, like congestive heart failure, tends to be associated with major Coenzyme Q10 deficiency. It may help to think of this relationship as a kind of chicken-egg phenomenon. Is this depletion state a direct result of the struggling heart's overconsumption of CoQ10 in cardiomyopathy, or does it represent the major risk factor in causing cardiomyopathy in the first place?

We know that CoQ10 administration improves myocardial mitochondrial function. Most of the research findings have been reported in terms of improved physical activity, change in clinical status or improved echocardiographic studies. Recently, low-dose CoQ10 for idiopathic (of unknown origin) dilated cardiomyopathy was reported in the *European Journal of Nuclear Medicine*.[26] In this small study of only 15 patients (14 men and 1 woman), only 30 mg of CoQ10 was administered for a period of approximately one month.

Investigators looked at whether or not functional changes in the heart could be detected by sophisticated nuclear imaging. The researchers, employing single photon emission tomography (SPET), were able to document and directly measure a significant therapeutic effect of Coenzyme Q10. Their research confirmed previous findings about the clinical effectiveness of CoQ10 supplementation as well as the appropriateness of metabolic SPET imaging as a way to measure the clinical impact of Coenzyme Q10. The results of this study also showed that even small dosages of CoQ10 could have significant implications for some patients with dilated cardiomyopathy.

HYPERTENSION

Systolic pressures in ranges of 140 to 150 mm/Hg and diastolic pressures greater than 90mm/Hg are detrimental to the heart and vascular system. Systolic pressure reflects the amount of pressure necessary to open the aortic valve for each contraction of the heart, and diastolic pressure is a measurement of the pressure or resistance (to blood flow) in the vascular bed, on the other side of the aortic valve against which the heart pumps. Diastolic pressure also reflects the amount of tone in the vascular walls that "milk" the blood through the arteries. These pressure levels, both systolic and diastolic, need to be balanced: high enough for optimum circulation and energy requirements, but not so high that excess wear and tear of the cardiovascular system occurs.

High Blood Pressure and CoQ10

Although the ability of CoQ10 to decrease blood pressure in experimental animal models was observed as early as 1972,[27] it was not until 1977 that Yamagami et al.[28] documented that actual CoQ10 deficiencies in hypertensive patients exist and that the administration of 1 to 2 mg/kg/day resulted in lowering blood pressure. Several years later, Yamagami conducted a follow-up, randomized, double-blind and controlled trial[29] on 20 hypertensive subjects with low serum CoQ10 levels.

Participants showed a significant decrease in both systolic and diastolic blood pressures after 12 weeks of a daily dose of 100 mg of CoQ10. Several other studies demonstrated similar findings at the same dose. In many of these studies, a minimum of four to twelve weeks of CoQ10 therapy was required before lowered blood pressure was realized.

The mechanism by which CoQ10 brings down high blood pressure is not fully understood.

In a recent study by Langsjoen and colleagues,[30] 109 patients with known hypertension were given 225 mg of CoQ10 daily, achieving a serum level of at least 2 ug/ml. There was a significant decrease in systolic blood pressure from an average of 159 mmHg down to 147 mmHg, while mean diastolic pressures dropped from 94 to 85 mmHg. In this study, the physician researchers were able to wean at least 50 percent of the subjects off one to three of their antihypertensive medications. My clinical experience in treating hypertension with CoQ10 has been parallel to the findings of Dr. Langsjoen's work. Since treating my patients with CoQ10 over the last decade, I have been able to slowly reduce at least half of their cardiac medications as well.

To avoid the many side effects of pharmacological drugs, I have developed a completely, natural, effective and easy-to-follow method for lowering blood pressure. My core program includes targeted nutritional supplementation that combines Coenzyme Q10 (usually up to 180 mg daily) with supplemental calcium, potassium and magnesium. When my patients have followed this program along with weight reduction via a healthy Mediterranean–style diet and low-level exercise, I have consistently been able to reduce their dosages of antihypertensive agents. Some have been able to discontinue drug therapy entirely.

The use of CoQ10 is a pivotal component of my core protocol to lower blood pressure. Although my clinical experience and that of the researchers is intriguing, the number of hypertensive patients in the investigation trials is relatively small. Large, multicentered, randomized studies should be performed to further evaluate and understand the role of Coenzyme Q10 in the treatment of systemic hypertension. High blood pressure remains the "silent killer" that represents a major health risk afflicting millions of people in this country; it also remains a major risk factor for cardiovascular disease. More research in this area is surely needed.

ANGINA

Angina is classically defined as a squeezing or pressure or even a burning-like chest pain. In simple terms, I refer to angina as a "heart cramp." It is caused by an insufficient supply of oxygen to the heart tissues, usually the result of blockages in the coronary arteries, which make the heart vulnerable. Intense cold, physical exertion, or even emotional stress may cause an increased need for oxygen and result in symptoms of angina. Spasm of the artery walls also contributes to a reduction in oxygen delivery. For some individuals, angina is the result of a combination of coronary artery spasm superimposed on underlying plaque. When angina is less predictable, with attacks occurring at random times, we say it has become "unstable" (also called Prinz-metal's angina). Basically, it comes down to cardiac economics: whatever the cause, the heart's *demand* for oxygen has outstripped the *supply*.

As a cardiologist, I do use medications to protect the heart muscle from the diminished oxygen supply. Some drugs work to reduce the heart's workload and oxygen demand by lowering blood pressure, heartrate or even myocardial over-contractility. Other medications, such as nitroglycerin, work directly on increasing the diameter of the arterial walls, which increases the supply of oxygen to the heart muscle. The effects of these agents may allow one to increase activity level without provoking anginal symptoms such as chest discomfort, shortness of breath, fatigue and so on. Most of the symptoms of angina are caused by atherosclerosis, a gradual buildup of cholesterol-laden plaque that usually progresses with age. Such a blockage tends to reduce the flow of oxygen to the heart muscle, thereby causing the symptoms of angina.

Drug therapy certainly has a definite place in the treatment of coronary artery disease, offering an improved quality of life in spite of coronary heart blockage. The major classes of drugs a cardiologist uses to reduce symptoms of coronary artery disease include nitrates, calcium channel blockers, beta blockers, ACE inhibitors and blood thinners such as aspirin.

As a cardiologist, I must recommend these drugs every day. However, although drugs have potential benefits, they also have variable, and sometimes unpleasant, side effects. I have treated many patients who are intolerant to one, or even all of these drugs. This is where Coenzyme Q10 comes in. It is a gift to cardiology.

CoQ10 and Angina

Coenzyme Q10 has been found to be effective in several small studies of patients with angina pectoris. In Japan Dr. Kamikawa and associates conducted a double-blind, cross-over-designed study of 12 patients with stable angina.[31]

The researchers documented that 150 mg daily of CoQ10

resulted in changes in three areas. Compared to placebo, treatment with Coenzyme Q10 was associated with:

- A reduction in the frequency of anginal episodes.
- A 54 percent decrease in the number of times nitroglycerine was needed to alleviate symptoms.
- An increased exercise time on treadmill testing.

There have also been several other small double-blind trials showing similar effects of the role of CoQ10 in coronary artery disease. In one multicentered study,[32] the effect of CoQ10 in doses of 150–300 mg a day was compared with placebo in 37 patients focusing on exercise duration at several centers. As in previous investigations, CoQ10 therapy correlated with an increase in exercise duration and a decrease in the frequency of anginal attacks.

In the 1994 study by Schardt, et al.,[33] 15 patients with chronic stable angina were enrolled in another double-blind crossover trial. Participants took 600 mg of CoQ10, placebo, or a combination of antianginal drugs (beta blockers and nitrates). Results of the three interventions were compared. Treatment with CoQ10 showed a significant reduction in exercise-induced electrocardiographic abnormalities on stress testing when compared to the placebo. There was no difference on the stress test EKGs when CoQ10 was compared to standard antianginal agents. In this study, a reduction in exercise systolic blood pressure was seen during CoQ10 supplementation, without any changes in diastolic blood pressure or heart rate.

Why exercise capacity is improved after CoQ10 administration is not fully understood. Several mechanisms are possible. First of all, CoQ10 has beneficial effects on oxidative phosphorylation, which is the process in which metabolic energy is released for cellular functions. Or perhaps CoQ10's antianginal action is the result of enhanced resynthesis of ATP, a direct membrane protection, a reduction in free radical stress or perhaps all of the above in combination. These CoQ10 properties are certainly different actions from those of conventional antianginal agents such as nitrates, beta blockers and calcium antagonists. Although large, placebo-controlled, randomized trials are needed to examine the anti-anginal effects of CoQ10, it is reasonable to administer CoQ10 to any patients who have an unsatisfactory quality of life despite conventional medical and surgical therapy and for those who have refractory angina.

When I treat people with angina, I recommend CoQ10 in a dose range of 90 to 360 mg in combination with antianginal agents, particularly for patients who have failed to get enough protection from conventional antianginal treatments. And because my patients have been able to enjoy the benefit of a more active lifestyle from CoQ10 supplementation, I believe it to be safe and effective treatment. With no significant adverse effects, CoQ10 is an exciting adjunct strategy for patients with angina pectoris.

ARRHYTHMIA

"Heart palpitations" are probably the most common complaint that brings people in to see me. Fortunately, irregular heartbeats are rarely a cause for concern; they occur in about one-third of all normal hearts.

One of the most common arrhythmias I see on the monitor are premature ventricular contractions (PVC's). Although a PVC may be experienced as a "skipped" heartbeat, it actually occurs earlier than the expected beat and is followed by a quick pause that feels as if a beat were missed. There are many causes for PVCs—stimulants like coffee, low potassium, alcohol, an aging conduction system, antiarrhythmic drugs, lack of oxygen, mitral valve prolapse and so on. The list is long. Most cardiologists do not use drugs to treat PVCs unless the individual is quite symptomatic. Before taking out my prescription pad for patients who have PVCs, I have them tested by echocardiogram, an ultrasound of the heart. If the test shows good heart function, then I use a nutritional approach for the arrhythmia, including CoQ10; the research findings are impressive.

CoQ10 and Arrhythmia

Mechanisms by which CoQ10 may act as an antiarrhythmic agent have been demonstrated in animal models. By stabilizing the membranes of the electrical conduction system, CoQ10 can make it harder for arrhythmias to start in the first place. It has been shown that CoQ10 causes a prolongation of action potential that can reduce the threshold for malignant ventricular arrhythmias in experimentally induced coronary ligation in dogs.[34, 35]

In an experimental study of rabbits[36] the experimental animals were given CoQ10 before a ligation procedure. Cellular mitochondria were then isolated 40 minutes after tying off a major blood vessel to the heart muscle. Higher levels of free radicals and lower levels of CoQ10 were identified. The effect of CoQ10 pretreatment was related to the degree of oxidative damage to the cells; destruction was reduced proportionate to pretreatment CoQ10 dosage.

When the blood vessel was reopened, radical stress in the placebo group was greater when compared to the group protected by CoQ10. This result has implications for the use of Coenzyme Q10 in cases where there is a surge in blood flow to the heart, such as in clot-dissolving therapy (thrombolysis) during an acute heart attack, angioplasty (PTCA) and coronary artery bypass surgery.

In one study of 27 patients[37] with premature ventricular ectopic beats, the reduction in PVC activity was significantly greater after four to five weeks of CoQ10 administration, 60 mg/day, than with placebo. Although the antiarrhythmic effect of CoQ10 was primarily seen in diabetics, a significant reduction in reports of palpitations was also noted for hypertensive and otherwise healthy patients.

This study also supports my own clinical experience. Similar research indicates Coenzyme Q10 treatment for PVCs is effective in approximately 20–25 percent[38] of patients. Additional research also shows that CoQ10 can have an effect in shortening the QT interval on the electrocardiogram.[39]

In a study of 61 patients admitted for acute heart attack, 32 subjects in the experimental group received 100 mg CoQ10 with 100 mcg selenium in the first 24 hours of hospitalization. This regimen was then maintained for one year. The control group of 29 patients received placebo over the same time period. The results were remarkable.

None of the participants in the experimental group showed prolongation of the QT interval, compared to 40 percent of control subjects, who had a mean QT increase of 440 msec (about 10 percent). Although there were no significant differences in early complications between the two groups, six (21 percent) of the control group died of recurrent heart attack, whereas one patient in the study group (3 percent) suffered a noncardiac death.[39] These study results suggest favorable CoQ10 effects on the ECG (reflecting membrane stabilization) which may have clinical and prognostic implications during the period after a heart attack, especially in patients vulnerable to ventricular arrhythmia.

The favorable effects of CoQ10 in reducing oxidative damage while reducing arrhythmia potential at the same time suggests CoQ10 as a logical choice in acute heart attack. Arrhythmia frequently occurs in the setting of a heart attack because the oxygen-deprived heart is electrically unstable and irritable cells in the conduction system can fire at random and run rampant. To date, I know of no randomized controlled trials that have evaluated CoQ10 for the prevention of cardiac arrhythmia in patients with acute heart attack. This will need further study. However, a 1996 study[40] did show protective benefit of antioxidants in acute heart attack; their usage was associated with a reduction in arrhythmia and even death. The same researchers are now performing a randomized trial of CoQ10 in patients with suspected heart attack. As you will see, since protective benefits of CoQ10 treatment were observed in the myocardial protection-cardiac surgery data, the use of CoQ10 in any case of acute coronary insufficiency—whether angina, heart attack, congestive heart failure, PTCA or CABG procedures—appears warranted.

MYOCARDIAL PROTECTION IN CARDIAC SURGERY

There have been numerous animal and human studies to investigate the possible protective benefit of pretreating surgical candidates with Coenzyme Q10. During cardiac operations, the body temperature is lowered to decrease metabolism. The body's blood supply is then rerouted onto the "bypass pump" so that the heart can be stilled for the surgery. The more limited the duration of this "pump time," the better.

Giving Coenzyme Q10 to pre-op cardiac patients has resulted in demonstrated improvement in right and left ventricular myocardial ultrastructure[41] when measured by light microscopy both pre- and postoperatively. Research has shown that pretreatment with CoQ10 is effective in preserving heart function following both CABG and valvular surgery.[42,43] As mentioned, experimental animal data has also confirmed that prior treatment with CoQ10 protects against ischemic reperfusion.[44]

The concept of reperfusion is quite intriguing. In reperfusion, oxygen-rich blood is delivered to an area of the heart that was previously denied adequate blood flow. Such reperfusion may be seen during the cardiac procedures described. Reperfusion of the heart muscle happens when a previously blocked artery vessel is unblocked after the surgeon applies a bypass, when the angioplasty cardiologist opens up a clogged vessel, or after a clot-busting agent is used to dissolve away the clot of a heart attack. Once good circulation has been reestablished by any of these methods, highly oxygenated blood can now rush in.

But the down side is that this fresh supply of oxygenated blood is delivered under high tension; now excessive oxygen is delivered to the starving tissues. All this oxygen must be broken down by the previously jeopardized cells, creating inevitable and harmful byproducts called reactive oxygen species (ROS).

This process can occur at such a fast pace that it can place an incredible oxidative stress on the tissue being rescued, setting the stage for what we call "reperfusion injury." It's analogous to throwing a life jacket to someone who's drowning, and then hitting them in the head with your rescue boat.

As mentioned earlier, CoQ10 has protective benefits before, during and after cardiac surgery. In one study, CoQ10 was administered to patients just before coronary artery bypass surgery. Their surgical outcomes were compared to control subjects who received no CoQ10. The CoQ10-treated patients had higher myocardial performance and lower requirements for cardiac drugs that help to support heart function while coming off heart-lung bypass.[43]

CORONARY ARTERY DISEASE (CAD) AND LIPID PEROXIDATION

Several studies have indicated that Coenzyme Q10, a lipid-soluble nutrient, acts as a potent antioxidant by inhibiting the process called lipid peroxidation (the oxidation of fats, including cholesterol and its components). Researchers at the Heart Research Institute in Sidney, Australia, have demonstrated a relationship between CoQ10 and circulating levels of low-density lipoproteins (LDLs). CoQ10 supplementation of 100 mg/three times a day for 11 days demonstrated increased resistance of LDL to the peroxidation process. In fact, the rate of LDL peroxidation was found to increase rapidly when CoQ10 levels were tapered down to 20 percent of their peak concentration.[45] This data has enormous implications, particularly since the oxidation of LDL appears to be the pivotal step in atherosclerosis.

Simple unoxidized LDL is harmless. But oxidized LDL is quickly picked up by endothelial cells and systemic monocytes, laying itself down on artery walls and irritating and inflaming underlying tissue, the foundation on which to build an atherosclerotic plaque. At this stage of proliferation, the oxidized LDL particle acts like a chemical magnet, attracting other monocytes, foam cells and building blocks for the fatty streak.

How can antioxidant activity block this dangerous cascade of events? Vitamin E (alpha tocopherol) and CoQ10, both powerful antioxidants, are known to be absorbed into the LDL package, a component of the cholesterol particle. Evidence has shown that once picked up by LDL, vitamin E can block LDL oxidation.

This has been observed *in vitro* (test tube serum) when oxidation is mediated by transition pro-oxidant metals.[46,47] Other vitamin researchers have documented that vitamin E supplementation increased vitamin E levels in LDL by 2.5 fold and reduced damaging lipid peroxidation of LDL by as much as 40 percent.[48] Knowing the level of vitamin E in the body may provide us a new and major predictor that can be evaluated and treated to accomplish the prevention of coronary artery disease. However, the synergistic relationship observed between vitamin E and Coenzyme Q10 is even more important.

The unique ability of CoQ10 to recycle vitamin E has tremendous treatment implications, especially since CoQ10 has also been shown to block lipid peroxidation.[49] CoQ10 exhibits its protective effect not only by scavenging free radicals, but by preventing the formation of oxidized LDL and boosting vitamin E stores as well. Some researchers believe that CoQ10 inhibits the oxidation of LDL cholesterol even more efficiently than vitamin E.[50,51]

ADVERSE REACTIONS

Adverse Events Reported for Long-term Usage of CoQ10 in 5,000 patients[1]

1. Epigastric discomfort (0.39%)
2. Decreased appetite (0.23%)
3. Nausea (0.16%)
4. Diarrhea (0.12%)
5. Elevated LDH (rare)
6. Elevated SGOT (rare)

I have been prescribing Coenzyme Q10 for over a decade and have not seen any significant adverse reactions despite the fact that many of my patients have taken hundreds of milligrams a day.

However, although I don't know of any absolute contraindications to CoQ10, I would not recommend it for pregnant women, nursing mothers, very young children or the newborn, since there is not yet enough data on its use in these populations.

DRUG INTERACTIONS

In all my years of experience with Coenzyme Q10, I have seen only a few major drug interactions. This is remarkable, especially since I use Coenzyme Q10 in combination with many cardiac drugs. In addition to the CoQ10-depleting effects of some cholesterol-lowering drugs, there are other drug interactions that have been reported.

For example, beta blockers have been shown to inhibit CoQ10-dependent enzymes. I have often wondered why occasional patients with congestive heart failure who take beta blockers have worsened. Was it due to Coenzyme Q10 depletion? Perhaps so. Although I frequently recommend Coenzyme Q10 and beta blockers for my patients, I am mindful about the CoQ10-depleting effects of these drugs.[2]

Coenzyme Q10 has also been known to reduce the drug-induced fatigue frequently experienced by people taking beta blockers.[3] Over the years, I have used Coenzyme Q10 in conjunction with beta blockers with much success, especially for the treatment of high blood pressure, arrhythmia and angina. The combination of CoQ10 and beta blockers works quite well in these situations.

Another group of drugs known to inhibit CoQ10-dependent enzymes is a class of psychotropic drugs including phenothiazines and tricyclic antidepressents.[4] I have often seen patients in my practice with arrhythmia, congestive heart failure and cardiomyopathy who have been taking these drugs over a long term. I also often wondered why an occasional patient develops cardiomyopathy and congestive heart failure on these drugs. Perhaps it was CoQ10 inhibition with impaired oxidative phosphorylation and ATP production, which may inhibit energy that supports myocardial contractility.

Even though many patients need to take these drugs in order to function in society, the concern about the cardiac effects of these drugs is warranted. Clinical studies have shown that Coenzyme Q10 supplementation results in improved EKGs in patients taking these psychoactive drugs. When I see patients in my practice who must take these medications but are having some cardiovascular side effects, I administer Coenzyme Q10 to help offset the possibility of these adverse effects.

Another area of potential concern is the use of Coenzyme Q10 in patients taking coumadin, a commonly prescribed blood thinner. Coumadin is commonly used to prevent blood clotting in atrial fibrillation, valvular problems and other medical problems where clot formation (embolus) is a concern. In 1994, the *Lancet*[5] reported three case studies where the reduced effect of coumadin was attributed to the use of CoEnzyme Q10. The reporting physician attributed this interaction to CoQ10, which he suggested had a vitamin K effect.

I have had patients on coumadin who ate foods high in vitamin K—like broccoli or spinach—the night before their bloodwork, and these foods also counteracted the coumadin and lowered their protimes (the time it takes the several clotting factors to form a clot). Changes in protimes may be related to diet, temperature changes and many other drugs. Thus, those on coumadin are always given dietary restrictions and should tell their physician if they are taking vitamin supplements and over-the-counter medications as well.

It may be that CoQ10 does slow the protime and so could have a blunting effect on coumadin therapy. This association should raise interest in performing a double-blind study to scientifically determine the effect of CoQ10 on protimes, controlling for all the other variables I mentioned.

New research indicates that CoQ10 may also reduce platelet stickiness, which could help prevent clot formation; a desirable effect for prevention of thrombicepisodes. I carefully monitor protimes in my patients on coumadin. If I feel that they need CoQ10 therapy as well, I know that I can always titrate the dose of each to keep both the symptoms and the protimes at therapeutic levels.

REFERENCES

Introduction
1. Tanaka, J., et al., Coenzyme Q10: The prophylactic effect of low cardiac output following cardiac valve replacement, *Ann Thorac Surg* 1982; 33:145–51.

CoQ10: A Miracle in our Midst

1. Frishman, W.H., et al., Innovative Pharmacologic Approaches for the Treatment of Myocardial Ischemia, In: Frishman, W.H., Sonnenblick, E.H., eds. *Cardiovascular Pharmaotherapeutics*. New York; McGraw-Hill 1997: 846–850.

History of CoQ10

1. Crane, F.L., et al., Isolation of a quinone from beef heart mitochondria. *Biochimica et Biophys. Acta*, 1957; 25:220–221.
2. Littarru, G.P., *Energy and Defense*. Rome, 14–24, 1195.
3. Littarru, G.P., Ho, L., and Folkers, K., Deficiency of Coenzyme Q10 in human heart disease. Part I and II. *Internat. J. Vit. Nutr. Res.*, 1972; 42(2):291:42(3)413.
4. Mitchell, P. Possible molecular mechanisms of the protonmotive function of cytochrome systems. *J. Theoret. Biol.*, 1976; 62:327–367.
5. Yamamura, Y. A survey of the therapeutic uses of Coenzyme Q in: Tenaz, G. (ed.): Coenzyme Q. John Wiley & Sons Ltd. New York, 492–493. 1985.
6. Langsjoen, P.H., Vadhanavikit, S. and Folkers, K. Response of patients in classes III and IV of cardiomyopathy to therapy in a blind and crossover trial with Coenzyme Q10. *Proc Natl Acad of Sci.* 1985; 82:4240–4244.
7. Ernster, L., and Forsmark, P. Ubiquinol: an endogenous antioxidant in aerobic organisms. Seventh International Symposium on Biomedical and Clinical Aspects of Coenzyme Q. Folkers, K., et al. (eds.) *The Clin Inves.* 1993; Suppl. 71(8):S60–S65.

Definition and Biochemistry of CoQ10

1. Littarru, G.P., *Energy and Defense*, Rome, 1995:14–24.
2. Greenberg, S. and Frishman, W.H., Coenzyme Q10: A new drug for cardiovascular disease, *Clin Pharm.* 1990; 30:596–608.
3. Kidd, P.M., et al. Coenzyme Q10: Essential Energy Carrier and Antioxidant. *HK Biomedical Consultants*, 1988; 1–8.
4. Miquel, J. Theoretical and experimental support for an "oxygen radical-mitochondrial injury" hypothesis of cell aging. In: Johnson J.E., et al. (eds.) *Free Radicals, Aging, and Degenerative Diseases*. New York: Aland R. Liss; 1986:51–55.
5. Smith, I.B., Ingerman, C.M. and Silver, M.J.: Malondialdehyde formation as an indicator of prostaglandin production by human platelets. *J. Lab Clin Med.* 1976; 88:167–72.
6. Porter, N.A.: Prostaglandin endoperoxides, In: Pryor, W.A., ed, *Free Radicals in Biology*, vol 4., London, Academic Press; 1980:261.
7. Stocker, R., Bowry, V.W., and Frei, B., Ubiquinol-10 protects human low density lipoproteins more efficiently against lipid peroxidation than does a-tocopherol. *Proc Natl Acad Sci USA* 1991; 88:1646–1650.
8. McGuire, J.J., et al., Succinate-ubiquinone reductase linked recycling of alpha-tocopherol in reconstituted systems and mitochondria: requirement for reduced ubiquinol. *Arch Biochem Biophys.* 1992; 292:47–53.
9. Serebruany, V.L., et al., Dietary Coenzyme Q10 supplementation alters platelet size and inhibits human bitronectin (CD51/CD61) receptor expression. *J Cardiovas Pharm.* 1997; 29:16–22.
10. Folkers, K., et al., The biomedical and clinical aspect of of Coenzyme Q, *Clin Investig.* 1993; 71:S51–S178.

How and When to Supplement with CoQ10

1. Kishi, T., et al., Serum levels of Coenzyme Q10 in patients receiving total paren-teral nutrition and relationship of serum lipids. In: Folkers, K. and Yamamura, Y. (eds.) *Biomedical and Clinical Aspects of Coenzyme Q.* 1986; 5:119.
2. Kalen, A., Appelkvist, E.L., Dallner, G.: Age-related changes in the lipid compo-sitions of rat and human tissues. *Lipids* 1989; 24:579–581.
3. Aryoma, O.I., Free Radicals and Antioxidant Strategies in Sports. *J Nutr Biochem* 1994; 5:370.
4. Ghirlanda, G., et al., Evidence of plasma CoQ10-lowering effect by HMG-CoA reductase inhibitors: A double-blind, placebo-controlled study. *J Clin Pharm* 1993; 33(3):226–9.
5. Folkers, K., et al., Lovastatin decreases Coenzyme Q10 levels in humans. *Proc Natl Acad Sci.* 1990; 87:8931–8934.
6. Folkers, K., et al., Evidence for a deficiency of Coenzyme Q10 in human heart disease, *Int J Vitam Nutr Res.* 1970; 40:380–90.
7. Littarru, G.P., Ho, L. and Folkers, K., Deficiency of coenzyme Q10 in human heart disease., *Int J Vitam Nutr Res.* 1972; 42:291–305.
8. Mancini, A., et al., Evaluation of metabolic status in Amiodarone-induced thy-roid disorders: Plasma Coenzyme Q10 determination, *J Endocrinol Invest.* 1989; 12:511–516.
9. Ernster, L., and Forsmark-Andre, P., Ubiquinol: An endogenous antioxidant in aerobic organisms, *Clin Investig.* 1993; 71:S62.
10. Hata T., Kunida H. and Oyama, Y., Antihypertensive effects of Coenzyme Q10 in essential hypertension, *Clin Endocrinol.* 1977; 25:1019–1022.
11. Maurer, I., Bernhard, A. and Zierz, S., Coenzyme Q10 and Respiratory Chain Enzyme Activities in Hypertrophied Human Left Ventricles with Aortic Valve Stenosis, *Am J Cardiol.* 1990; 66:504–505.
12. Hanaki, Y., Coenzyme Q10 and coronary artery disease, *Clin Invest.* 1993; 71:S112–S115.
13. Yoshida, T., Maulik, G. Increased myocardial tolerance to ischemia-reperfusion injury by feeding pigs with Coenzyme Q10, *Ann NY Acad Sci.* 1996; 793:414–418.
14. Folkers, K., Perspectives from research on vitamins and hormones, *J Chem Educ.* 1984; 61:747–56.
15. Folkers, K., Vadhanavikit, S. and Mortensen, S.A., Biochemical rationale and myocardial tissue data on the effective therapy of cardiomyopathy with Coen-zyme Q10, *Proc Natl Acad Sci. USA* 1985; 82(3):901–904.
16. Sinatra, S., CoQ10 formulation can influence bioavailability, *Nutrition Science News* 1997; 2(2):88.
17. Chopra, R. et al.: Relative bioavailability of Coenzyme Q10 formulations in human subjects. *International Journal for Vitamin and Mineral Research* 1997.
18. Lansjoen, P.H., et al., Long-term efficacy and safety of Coenzyme Q10 therapy for idiopathic dilated cardiomyopathy, *Am J Cardiol.* 1990; 65:512–23.
19. Proceedings from the 9th International Conference on CoQ10, Ancona, 1996.

Coenzyme Q10 in Clinical Cardiovascular Disease

1. Folkers, K., Vadhanavikit, S. and Mortensen, S.A., Biochemical rationale and myocardial tissue data on the effective therapy of cardiomyopathy with Coen-zyme Q10, *Proc Natl Acad Sci. USA.* 1985; 82(3):901–904.
2. Kamikawa, T., et al., Effects of Coenzyme Q10 on exercise tolerance in chronic stable angina pectoris, *Am J Cardiol.* 1985; 56:247–251.

3. Kuklinski, B., Weissenbacher, E. and Fahnrich, A., Coenzyme Q10 and antioxidants in acute myocardial infarction. *Mol Aspects Med.* 1994; 15 Suppl: s143–7.
4. Hanaki, Y., Coenzyme Q10 and coronary artery disease, *Clin Invest.* 1993; 71:S112–S115.
5. Greenberg SM, and Frishman, W.H., Coenzyme Q10: A new drug for cardiovascular disease, *Clin Pharm.* 1990; 30:596–608.
6. Hata, T., Kunida, H. and Oyama, Y., Antihypertensive effects of Coenzyme Q10 in essential hypertension, *Clin Endocrinol.* 1977; 25:1019–1022.
7. Digiesi, V., Cantini, F., and Brodbeck, B., Effect of Coenzyme Q10 on essential arterial hypertension, *Current Therapeutic Research.* 1990; 47:841–845.
8. Domac, N., et al., Cardiomyopathy and other chronic toxic effects induced in rabbits by doxorubicin and possible prevention by Coenzyme Q10, *Cancer Treat Rep.* 1981; 65(1–2):79–91.
9. Takahashi, K., Mayumi, T. and Kiski, T., Influence of Coenzyme Q10 on doxorubicin uptake and metabolism by mouse myocardial cells in culture, *Chem Pharm bull.* 1988; 36:1514–1518.
10. Langsjoen, P.H., Vadhanavikit, S. and Folkers, K., Response of patients in classes III and IV of cardiomyopathy to therapy in a blind and crossover trial with Coenzyme Q10, *Proc Natl Acad of Sci.* 1985; 82:4240–4244.
11. Hoffman-Bang, C., et al., Coenzyme Q10 as an adjunctive in treatment of congestive heart failure, *Am J of Cardiol.* 1992 Supplement 19(3),216A.
12. Morisco, C., Trimarco, B. and Condorelli, M., Effect of coenzyme Q10 therapy in patients with congestive heart failure: A long-term multicenter randomized study. In: Folkers, K., et al., (eds.), Seventh International Symposium on Biomedical and Clinical Aspects of Coenzyme Q, *The Clinical Investigator.* 1993; 71:S134–S136.
13. Manzoli, U., et al: Coenzyme Q10 in dilated cardiomyopathy, *Int J Tissue React.* 1990; 12:173–8.
14. Judy, W.V., Folkers, K. and Hall, J.H., Improved long-term survival in Coenzyme Q10-treated chronic heart failure patients compared to conventionally treated patients, *Biomedical and Clinical Aspects of CoEnzyme Q.* eds. K. Folkers, G. P. Littarru and T. Yamagami, Vol 6, 1991; 291–298.
15. Langsjoen P.H. and Folkers, K., Isolated diastolic dysfunction of the myocardium and its response to CoQ10 treatment, *Clin Invest.* 1993; 71:S140–S144.
16. Pogessi, L., et al., Effect of Coenzyme Q10 on left ventricular function in patients with dilated cardiomyopathy, *Current Therapy and Research.* 1991; 49:878–886.
17. Baggio, E., et al., Italian multicenter study on safety and efficacy of Coenzyme Q10, *The Molecular Aspects of Medicine.* 1994; 15:S287–S294.
18. Folkers, K. et al: Evidence for a deficiency of Coenzyme Q10 in human heart disease, *Int J Vitam Nutr Res.* 1970; 40:380–90.
19. Littarru, G.P., Ho, L. and Folkers, K., Deficiency of Coenzyme Q10 in human heart disease I., *Int J Vitam Nutr Res.* 1972; 42:291–305.
20. Folkers, K., Perspectives from research on vitamins and hormones, *J Chem Educ.* 1984; 61:747–56.
21. Langsjoen, P.H. et al: Long-term efficacy and safety of Coenzyme Q10 therapy for idiopathic dilated cardiomyopathy. *Am J Cardiol.* 1990; 65:512-23.
22. Langsjoen, P.H.., Langsjoen, P. and Folkers, K., Isolated diagnostic dysfunction of the myocardium and its response to CoQ10 treatment, *Clin Invvest.* 1993; 71(8):S140–4.
23. Langsjoen, P.H., Langsjoen, P., Willis, R. Folkers, K.: usefulness of coenzyme Q10 in clinical cardiology: A long-term study. *Mol Aspects Med.* 1994; 15:S165–75.

24. Soja, A.M. and Mortensen, S.A., Treatment of congestive heart failure with Coenzyme Q10 illuminated by meta-analyses of clinical trials, *Molecular Aspects of Medicine.* 1997; 18:S159–S168.
25. Sinatra, S.T.: Refractory congestive heart failure successfully managed with high-dose Coenzyme Q10 administration, *Molecular Aspects of Medicine.* 1997; 18:S299–S305.
26. Kim, Y., et al., Therapeutic effect of Coenzyme Q10 on idiopathic dilated cardiomyopathy: Assessment by iodine-123 labelled 15-(p-iodophenyl)-3(R,S)-methylpentadecanoic acid myocardial single-photon emission tomography, *European Journal of Nuclear Medicine.* 1997; 24:629–634.
27. Igarashi, T., et al., Effect of Coenzyme Q10 on experimental hypertension in the desoxycorticosterone acetate-saline loaded rats, *Folic Pharm Jap.* 1972; 68:460.
28. Yamagami, T., Shibata, N. and Folkers, K., Study of Coenzyme Q10 in essential hypertension. In: Folkers, K. and Yamamura, Y. (eds.). *Biomedical and Clinical Aspects of Coenzyme Q10*, Vol. 1. Amsterdam: Elsevier, 1977:231–242.
29. Yamagami, T. et al., Effect of Coenzyme Q10 on essential hypertension: A double-blind controlled study. In: Folkers, K. and Yamamura, Y. (eds.), *Biomedical and Clinical Aspects of Coenzyme Q*, Vol 5, Elsevier Sci Publ B.V. Amsterdam, 1986; 337–343.
30. Langsjoen, P., Willis, R. and Folkers, K., Treatment of essential hypertension with Coenzyme Q10. *Mol Aspects Med.* 1994; 15 (suppl):265–272.
31. Kamikawa, T., et al., Effects of Coenzyme Q10 on exercise tolerance in chronic stable angina pectoris, *Am J Cardiol.* 1985; 56:247–251.
32. Wilson, M.R., et al., Coenzyme Q10 therapy and exercise duration in stable angina. In: Folkers, K., Littarru, G.P. and Yamagami, T., (eds)., *Biomedical and Clinical Aspects of Coenzyme Q*, Vol. 6, Amsterdam; Elsevier, 1991:339–348.
33. Schardt, F., et al., Effect of Coenzyme Q10 on ischemia-induced ST-segment depression: A double-blind placebo-controlled crossover study. In: Folkers, K. and Yamamura, Y; (eds.), *Biomedical and Clinical Aspects of Coenzyme Q*, Vol 5. Amsterdam: Elsevier 1986: 385–394.
34. Nogai, S. et al., The effect of Coenzyme Q10 on reperfusion injury in canine myocardium, *J Mol Cell Cardiol.* 1985; 17:873–878.
35. Husono, K. et al., Protective effects of Coenzyme Q10 against arrhythmia and its intracellular distribution. A study on the cultured single myocardial cell. In: Folkers, K. and Yamamura, Y. (eds.), *Biomedical and Clinical Aspects of Coenzyme Q10*, Vol. 3, Elsevier/North Holland Biomedical Press, Amsterdam, 1981:269–278.
36. Otani, T. et al., In vitro study on contribution of oxidative metabolism of isolated rabbit heart mitochondria to myocardial reperfusion injury, *Circ Res.* 1984; 55:168–175.
37. Fujioka, T. Sakamoto, Y. and Mimura, G., Clinical study of cardiac arrhythmias using a 24-hour continuous electrocardiographic recorder (5th report)-Antiarrhythmic action of Coenzyme Q10 in diabetes. *Tohoku J Exp Med.* 1983; 141(Suppl):453–463.
38. Ohnishi, S., et al., The effect of Coenzyme Q10 on premature ventricular contraction. In: Folkers, K. and Yamamura, Y., (eds.) *Biomedical and Clinical Aspects of Coenzyme Q10*, Vol. 5. Elsevier Sci. Publ. B.V., Amsterdam, 1986:257–266.
39. Kuklinski, B., Weissenbacher, E. and Fahnrich, A. Coenzyme Q10 and antioxidants in acute myocardial infarction. *Mol Aspects Med.* 1994; 15(suppl): S143–S147.
40. Singh, R.B., et al., Usefulness of antioxidant vitamins in suspected acute myocardial infarction (the Indian experiment of infarct survival-3), *Am J of Cardiol* 1996; 77:232–236.

41. Chen, Y.F., Lin, Y.T. and Wu, S., Effectiveness of Coenzyme Q10 on myocardial preservation during hypothermic cardioplegic arrest, *J thorac Cardiovas Surg.* 1994; 107:242–7.
42. Sunamori, M., et al., Clinical experience of CoQ10 to enhance interoperative myocardial protection in coronary artery revascularization, *Cardiovasc Drug Therapy* 1991; 5 Suppl 2:297–300.
43. Tanaka, J. et al., Co-enzyme Q10: The prophylactic effect of low cardiac output following cardiac valve replacement, *Ann Thorac Surg.* 1982; 33:145–51.
44. Nayler, W.G., The use of Coenzyme Q10 to ischaemia heart muscle. In: Yamamura, Y., Folkers, K. and Ito, Y., (eds.): *Biomedical and Clinical Aspects of Coenzyme Q10,* Vol. 2, Elsevier, North Holland. Biomedical Press, Amsterdam, 1980:409–425.
45. Mohr, D., Bowry, W.W. and Stocker, R., Dietary supplementation with Coenzyme Q10 results in increased levels of ubiquinol-10 within circulating lipidprotein and increased resistance of human low-density lipoprotein to the initiation of lipid peroxidation, *Biochim Biophys Act* 1992; 1126:247–254.
46. Morel, D.W., Hessler, J.R. and Chisolm, G.M., Low-density lipoprotein cytotoxicity induced by free radical peroxidation of lipid, *J Lipid Res* 24:1070–6.
47. Esterbaurer, H., et al., Continuous monitoring of *in vitro* oxidation of human low-density lipoproteins, *Free Rad Res Commun* 1989; 6:67–75.
48. Reaven, P. et al: Effect of dietary antioxidant combinations in humans, *Arterioscler Thromb* 1993; 13:590–600.
49. Frei, B., Kim, M.C. and Ames, B.N., Ubiquinol-10 is an effective lipid-soluble antioxidant at physiological concentrations. *Proc Natl Acad Sci, USA* 1990; 87:48–79–4883.
50. Bowry, V.W., et al., Prevention of tocopherol-mediated peroxidation in ubiquinol-10-free human low-density lipoprotein. *J Biol Chem* 1995; 270(11):5756–63.
51. Ingold, K.U., et al., Autoxidation of lipids and antioxidation by alpha-tocopherol and ubiquinol in homogeneous solution and in aqueous dispersions of lipids: Unrecognized consequences of lipid particle size as exemplified by oxidation of human low-density lipoprotein, *Proc Natl Acad Sci, USA* 1993; 90(1):45–49.

Adverse Reactions

1. Greenberg, S. and Frishman, W.H., Coenzyme Q10: A new drug for cardiovascular disease, *Clin Pharm.* 1990; 30:596–608.
2. Kishi, T., Kishi, H., and Folkers, K., Inhibition of cardiac CoQ10-enzymes by clinically used drugs and possible prevention. In: *Biomedical and Clinical Aspects of Coenzyme Q10,* Vol 1. Folkers, K. and Yamamura, Y. (eds.). Elsevier/North-Holland Biomedical Press, Amsterdam, 1977, pp. 47–62.
3. Hamada, M., Kazatani, Y., Ochi, T., et al., Correlation between serum CoQ10 level and myocardial contractility in hypertensive patients. In: *Biomedical and Clinical Aspects of Coenzyme Q10, Vol 4.* Folkers, K. and Yamamura, Y. (eds.). Elsevier Science Publ, Amsterdam, 1984, pp. 263–270.
4. Kishi, T., et al., Inhibition of myocardial respiration by psychotherapeutic drugs and prevention by coenzyme Q. In: *Biomedical and Clinical Aspects of Coenzyme Q10, Vol 2.* Yamamura Y., Folkers K. and Ito Y (eds.). Elsevier/North-Holland Biomedical Press, Amsterdam, 1980, pp. 139–154.
5. Spigset, O. Reduced effect of warfarin caused by ubidecarenone. In: *The Lancet, Vol 344; 1994:1372–1373.*